REMEMBERING THE MAN AND HIS VISION

by Irose Fernella Thompson

With excerpts from
Bishop James O. Thompson's writings
dated April 7, 1978

ENDORSEMENTS

I can remember Dr. Thompson saying, "Young People, get your education. No one can take that away from you." I listened to him, and then followed in his footsteps to advance in education.

Ember Levine – Dixon West Orange, New Jersey

Bishop James O. Thompson was a man of integrity, filled with the Holy Ghost. He loved people, believed in the vision that God gave him, "Evangelism through Education," which led him to open TET Christian Academy.

Deacon Chester Banks,
Dean of the Jersey City Bible School;
Principal Audrey Banks of TET Christian Academy,
Jersey City, New Jersey

Dr. James Thompson was an extraordinary man who had a commitment for souls and was very dedicated to the ministry. In spite of opposition, he remained faithful to the vision. His physical presence is gone; however, his spirit rests with us forever.

Deacon Christopher Watkins;
Missionary Terry Watkins, Truth Evangelistic Temple,
Jersey City, New Jersey

iii

Bishop James Thompson demonstrated what Jesus commands His followers to do in Matthew 5:16. His life exemplified that "light" of love, joy, peace, patience, gentleness, goodness, faith, meekness and self-control. We enjoyed a working relationship with him.

Dr. Aldansa Ambrose, pastor of Grace Hill Tabernacle, and Dr. Ellen Ambrose, Newark, New Jersey

Bishop James Thompson was a man who loved God and His Word, and his family and friends. He also enjoyed teaching others. He had a mind to fulfill the vision God gave him to the end of his life.

Bishop Howard Scales, MD

Dr. James Thompson was a mentor; he was sincere and very truthful. He presented himself friendly, was always challenging mentally and spiritually. It is not by accident that he named the church Truth Evangelistic Temple; that is what he preached, lived and taught.

Elder Tall Johnson, Jersey City, New Jersey

The late Bishop Thompson's memory stands out in my mind; special moments include times spent at his home between church services. Two of his quotes stand out very vividly in my thoughts, "All shut eyes are not sleep, and all good byes are not gone." This was his rational for taking his naps. After each sermon he would also say, "If you don't have a desire to a live right, you don't need a church home." He is greatly missed.

Michelle Adams, Bayonne, New Jersey

Bishop James O. Thompson inspired us to become leaders by promoting harmony and teamwork, and by committing himself with a high degree of honesty, loyalty and integrity. We are truly blessed to have shared time, love, tears and joy with this great man of God who has greatly touched our lives.

Sister Regina Campbell and family,
Jersey City, New Jersey

DEDICATION

To the loving memory of my late husband, Bishop – Dr. James Oliver Thompson, Sr.

To his four children: Michael, James Jr. (Jimmy), Clarence Thompson and Mrs. Carolyn Lawrence, and step-son, Virgil Roberts, Jr.

To his grandchildren, to his brothers, sisters, nieces, nephews, in-laws, friends and well-wishers.

To the Truth Evangelistic Temple Church family and TET Christian Academy, staff and students that he nourished and cherished during his lifetime.

God richly bless you.

ACKNOWLEDGEMENTS

To my pastor, Elder Je'vah Richardson, and shepherd of our flock at Truth Evangelistic Temple, 695 Ocean Avenue, Jersey City, New Jersey, for his love and continued support during the loss of my husband.

To the assistant pastor, Elder Wayne Lawrence, for lending an ear, and for his support.

To my son, Virgil Roberts Jr., and his wife, Yolander, and their children, for their continued love and support.

To my mother, Mrs. Mary Adams-Davis, for being here, just when I needed her most.

To my sisters, Rosaly and Michelle Adams, who stood faithfully with me, along with my other siblings.

To my stepson, James Jr. (Jimmy), and his loving wife, Ninetta, for checking up on me.

To my brothers and sisters in-law in North Carolina.

To my step-grandchild, Teyona Thompson, for her loving embrace and support.

To my spiritual mother, Lucy Davis, for her prayers and support.

To my friends, Pastor Sylvia Dadie, Evangelist Glendia Cannon, Mrs. Daphne Fingal, Evangelist Ellen Ambrose, Pastor Lula Haas, for their prayers and continued support.

To my spiritual daughters, Sister Lucinda Dupree, Sister Takia Campbell, for their love and support.

To my loving adoptive daughter, Mrs. Paula Smart, who supports me all the way.

To these mothers of TET church: Mother Jewel Cody, who is very supportive, Mothers Elizabeth Curry and Mother Ann Pennington for their love and support.

To all the brothers and sisters of Truth Evangelistic Temple for their love and support.

Special thanks to the following clergy and their wives:

Bishop and Mother Commodore, Neptune, NJ.

Bishop Dr. Thomas Robinson and Evangelist Rose Robinson, Bayonne, NJ.

Bishop James Heron and Mother Rose Heron, Jersey City, NJ.

Bishop Dr. Elroy Benn and Co-Pastor Delores Benn, Newark, NJ.

Bishop Wayman Wright and Mother Wright, Jersey City, NJ.

Dr. Richard Green and Sister Green, Jersey City, NJ.

Dr. Tall Johnson and Sister Johnson, Jersey City, NJ.

Dr. Aldansa Ambrose and Evangelist Ellen Ambrose, NJ.

Dr. Nathaniel Screvens and Evangelist Screvens, Newark, NJ.

Drs. Frank Gregory and Evangelist Gregory, Jersey City, NJ.

Elder Henry Cannon and Evangelist Glendia Cannon, Jersey City, NJ.

Elder John Milligan, Jersey City, NJ.

Elder Erick Robinson, Bayonne, NJ.

Elder William Stathom and Mother Stathom, Jersey City, NJ.

Elder Bobby Roberson and Missionary Carrie Roberson, Garfield, GA.

Rev. Mary Milligan, Jersey City, NJ.

Elder Lee Watson and Sister Watson, Jersey City, NJ.

Pastor Dadie Sylvia, Newark, NJ.

Pastor Lula Hass, Newark, NJ.

Elder Collins and Sister Collins, Jersey City, NJ.

Rev. Mother Underhill, East Orange, NJ.

TABLE OF CONTENTS

Introduction

An Old Country Preacher

Presenting *Remembering the Man and His Vision* gives me a bit of satisfaction, and an exuberance of knowing this individual whose character and reference stand out so beautifully. Dr. James Thompson was a man of integrity, humility, compassion, knowledge, wisdom and understanding, coupled with love. These traits brought out his personality, even through his bouts with sickness.

Dr. Thompson's humble spirit was one of the factors noted; all the degrees, awards and various accomplishments did not change his persona. He was very careful to say, as he referred to himself, "I am an old country preacher." His other saying was, "One can have all these degrees, and still go to Hell."

He held a deep compassion for souls; not only the spiritual aspect, he was also concerned with the physical. I can remember him saying, "Sweetie, a pastor's job is not an easy one." At times, I could actually feel the pain emanating from within.

One of my husband's greatest desires was to pen his life story – certain advantages and disadvantages he faced as he embraced the vision given to him by God. In detailed discussions with him, I learned that the thought of being a foster child tormented his mind. Another giant that he had to face was in the area of education, which he pursued very passionately. He became knowledgeable biblically and in the secular field, earning various awards and degrees. He wanted to leave a blueprint for other young people who may be faced with the same struggles, to let them know that there is a way out of their dilemma.

This book will include excerpts from Bishop Thompson's own writings, labeled "Material for My Book." These writings came from his thesis, marked "Psychology of Religious Development, James O. Thompson, term paper, dated: April 7, 1978." He was trying to come up with a title.

WRITE MY BOOK

After he took ill, he said to me, "Sweetie, you are going to have to write my book. I want you to tell my story." This became embedded in my mind.

After his death, I prayed for a title and God, through the person of His blessed Holy Spirit, birthed this title in my spirit: *Remembering the Man and His Vision.*

The words of the minor prophet Habakkuk began to stir up in my spirit, "For the vision is yet for an appointed time, but at the end it shall speak, and not lie: though it tarry, wait for it: because it will surely come; it will not tarry" (Habakkuk 2:3).

I had embraced Dr. Thompson's vision after marrying him, December 11, 1999. Now his vision lives on through many facts. He became an icon for evangelism through education. He believed in his conviction, which he adhered to faithfully.

This book will expose the dynamic overall magnitude of this man's life and vision, a vision which withstood the test of time. He wrote a last note on his pad, just before the ambulance came, and it reads thus:

"I am who God says I am,

I can do what God says I can do."

He was truly a loving father, husband, friend; most of all a God-fearing man who stands for the truth.

Irose Fernella Thompson

CHAPTER ONE

It Is a Question of "Why?"

Sitting in my straight-back red chair, I can recall many conversations my husband and I had over the years. As he sat in his chair, slumped forward at times, he usually spoke between naps, as he related some of his fears and thoughts of being rejected during childhood. The memories of certain events troubled him, where he asked the question, "Why?" Here, in his own words, he relates his story from the beginning.

AN OPEN WOUND

I was reared in North Carolina with foster parents. Both were illiterate: neither could even read nor write, not even their names. My foster brother and I both dropped out of school. I finished the seventh grade in a school where anyone could teach. I can only vaguely remember attending church a couple of times in my life, but somehow we were religious. My foster mother taught the siblings about God, even though she could not read. The teachings were not in depth, she was only able to teach a hearsay religion.

His foster mother was a strict disciplinarian, never sparing the rod; her husband was a gun-toting father who drank liquor freely. My husband joked about wearing his overalls and high-top rubber boots to protect him from snake bites. He spoke about the fact that when he should have been in school, he would be sent to the cotton fields to clean the cotton. We both joked about Dyfus (Division of Youth and Family Services) and wondered if they were active in those days; if they had been, the foster parents would have been investigated. There was s sense of an open wound still present which needed healing.

At times our discussions opened up the door for further ventilation; most of the time, they were a mixture of laughter and empathy as we opened the pages of our lives: the pendulum swings, then chimes.

THE MATTER OF EDUCATION

After 16 years of farm life I decided to go into the army; I was 16, this was back in the forties. After completing two years of army life, I returned to civilian life, uneducated and broke. Afterwards I married a well-educated girl who bore four beautiful children for me; then after ten years of marriage. I was finally convinced to go back to school.

As the matter of his education became more and more prevalent in his thoughts, he began to pursue his high school diploma by taking courses and reading books. This journey meant a lot to him, it was a beginning of a new chapter in his life. He had to juggle his way, being a husband, father and now a student.

CHAPTER TWO

The Turning Point

After frequenting the bars and the gambling games, he told me that he was hitting rock bottom. A change had to come about. He felt a desire burning in the inside; something was getting a hold of him, he could not resist it anymore.

The real change in my depleted and exhausted life came when I returned to the church (I had never really been in the church). On this return trip I was really seeking the Lord in His fullness. I really wanted to be saved, though the term saved was not used or heard of back in the early forties or fifties as it is today. It was strictly a term that identified with the Pentecost, Holiness, or Apostolic Doctrines. In 1955, I gave my heart to the Lord. There I worked in every department of the church. In 1959 I received the gift of the Holy Spirit, with the initial evidence of speaking in tongues, as God gives the utterance. This belief finds its origin on the day of Pentecost in the Upper Room.

100 PERCENT CHANGE

He explained to me that his conversion took place in a midweek service, and after that he never touched alcohol or smoked another cigarette. His gambling crew missed him; they could not understand what had taken place. The Apostle Paul explains it in this Scripture:

> *Therefore if any man be in Christ, he is a new creature: old things are passed away; behold, all things are become new.*
>
> (2 Corinthians 5:17)

He made a 100 percent change in his life because, first of all, of the conviction of the Spirit showing him his faults; secondly, he had a mind to turn. We talked about rehabilitation; he never went to rehab. The Holy Ghost did a thorough work on him and the appetite for these substances was dried up.

The whole impact of his childhood ordeal enhanced his momentum to persevere with his plan of educating himself. He was determined not to build walls that he could not penetrate. In reality, the walls could not detain him; he had to find a way to break down those walls. It was as if he had a "Jericho experience" in order for him to get to his "Promised Land," which in this case was the "vision."

There was some tearing down which had to take place.

DIRECTIONS TO THE DESTINATION

Joshua was given specific instructions from God on how to conquer Jericho. Likewise, Bishop Thompson's inspiration of how to get to his destination was given to him by God. He was not able to grasp the full content until he surrendered to God.

Many times we ask the Lord to show us the way; we want directions in order for us to get to the place that has been predestined for us. I truly believe that the full manifestation of God's plans for our lives will not be revealed until we find ourselves in that place where we are ready to receive.

One day in conversation he talked about how his life was like a "roller coaster"; a great majority of us can identify as such. On that ride, we meet many bumps and rough spots. The Word of God should always be our measuring tape. The Apostle Paul gives us this answer:

> *We are troubled on every side, yet not distressed; we are perplexed, but not in despair; persecuted, but not forsaken; cast down, but not destroyed.*
> (2 Corinthians 4:8-9)

We are oftentimes puzzled as we struggle with the things that confront us daily. Our emotions sometimes get the best of us. As a child of God, Bishop was at a place of "finding himself." Some of us may require a longer period while others can get there faster.

CHAPTER THREE

From a Farmboy to a Country Preacher

FURTHER EDUCATION

After turning his life over to God, Bishop was determined to carry out the "Great Commission," and he also purposed in his mind that every student deserves the right to have access to education.

It was this new experience that motivated me back to school. In 1962, I was called into the ministry. Amongst the blacks a person can have been or have done a little of everything, and yet be called into the ministry of Christ. However, there was a discontentment in my life, for I believed that God wanted His people to know, to be educated. Although many of my black ancestors never got out of grammar school, they won thousands of souls to Christ. They also built two and three hundred thousand dollar buildings for God. In me there was an inner voice which told me that soci-

ety was heading for a more enlightened structure, and if the black ministers were going to keep up with their segments of people, they too needed to be educated to deal with the next generation of blacks.

After I finished high school I attended Bible College to get my biblical training, then I grasped for more knowledge. I attended Rutgers University, where I majored in sociology, and then I continued on to graduate school.

Psychologically, I see myself as a fairly broad-minded person with some inner conflicts relating to my past and present. In conflicts relating to the past, I see myself as a person deprived, stripped and bereaved of an education early in my boyhood, which continued until manhood. Education has become my goal in life.

I had for my many years despised the South and its representatives as a whole for depriving me of my privilege to get an education. It was not until I had given my heart to the Lord and began to educate myself that I lost that feeling of hostility toward the South and its representatives. I now learn and realize that it is not how much education a person has, it is what he does constructively with the knowledge.

Bishop told me that having to take care of his family, attending school, then being a full-time pastor, was "blood, sweat, and tears." He worked faithfully to earn his degrees, which includes: Associate in Science from Essex County College in Newark, New Jersey on May 6, 1973; his Bachelor of Theology on June 2, 1968, and his Master of Theology on June 7, 1070 from Divinity School; a Master of Science, from Iona College, New York in February 1984; a Bachelor of Arts at Rutgers University, in Newark, NJ, in

June, 1975; in addition to Doctoral Degrees from Jamison College and Manhattan Bible College.

SURRENDERING THE WILL

He experienced hardships during these periods yet he held on to his integrity and surrendered his will and his way to God, which is very important for any leader. The lines of communication must be kept open in order to hear God's voice.

I have set myself up as a savior for the uneducated people; by that statement I meant to encourage them to go back to school. I also realized that college is not for everyone, they would have to make that choice when the opportunity presented itself. I have a great deal of satisfaction to know that if I have inspired someone to stay in or return to school, that is a big step.

In 1962, Bishop preached his first sermon in the capacity of a minister; each time he would tell this story, there was a glow which emanated from his face. His topic: "Pattern of a Would-be Christian."

September 4, 1966, he was ordained by the Bible Way Church of Christ, worldwide, to the office of Elder. It must also be noted that he came up through the ranks in his church, where he held various offices such as: usher, board president, deacon, praise and worship leader, etc. Consistency and punctuality were two of his most valued traits when it comes to God's business; these were very important to him amongst others. He shared times when he would sweep, mop the floor, and paint the walls of the church. As he looked back, and saw how far God had brought him, he would say, "Thank You, Lord."

CHAPTER FOUR

The Conception

And he gave some, apostles; and some, prophets; and some, evangelists; and some, pastors and teachers; for the perfecting of the saints, for the work of the ministry, for the edifying of the body of Christ: till we all come in the unity of the faith, and of the knowledge of the Son of God, unto a perfect man, unto the measure of the stature of the fulness of Christ.

(Ephesians 4:11-13)

NURTURING THE VISION

After my husband received the gift of the Holy Ghost (Spirit) in 1959, he became impregnated with a "vision" from God, which is "Evangelism through Education." He cherished that vision more than anything else that came his way.

After returning home from the military he moved to New Jersey, working in different jobs such as: a die cutter, a cartoonist, carpentry and photography. There was something in him that had to be nurtured.

"Conception" in the natural means that the mother has conceived and she must take care of her body, eat right, get plenty of rest, etc. In spiritual conception, there is a particular vision that God has given to the person; they in turn have to nurture the vision and see to it that it does not get aborted.

Bishop continued to seek the Lord's face as to how this vision was coming to manifestation.

> *And the Lord answered me, and said, Write the vision, and make it plain upon tables, that he may run that readeth it. For the vision is yet for an appointed time, but at the end it shall speak, and not lie: though it tarry, wait for it; because it will surely come, it will not tarry.*
> (Habakkuk 2:2-3)

First, he had to have the vision written in his heart, realizing that it was for an appointed time, which God had in store for its manifestation. He continued to pray, fast and meditate on the Word of God. He told me that the vision was given to him in plain dimensions. After living through certain circumstances in his life, it was time for him to pave the way for others.

CHAPTER FIVE

The Birthing Process

After he was consecrated an Elder by the Bible Way Church of Christ September 4, 1966, Truth Evangelism Temple Church was birthed. Amongst his first members were his late wife, Henrietta and his four children, along with three others. This is what he said to me, "I remembered when some young people walked in from off the street, desiring to join the choir." He was concerned as to what their parents would say.

The young people were very elated; they became a part of the choir which is known as the "The Thompsonettes." After 39 years, some are still a member of the choir today.

EXPANDING THE VISION

Bishop had a special affection for young people; in other words, he saw the vision unfolding. He related a feeling of sadness when one would leave. The members fluctuated off and on; many went on to be pastors or teachers, while others relocated.

The Jersey City Bible Institute and Christian Counseling was another expansion of the vision. He told me about the many trials that he went through as he pursued the vision.

My mountain had been a part of my life and personality ever since I came into accountability. I have stood at the bottom of this enormous gigantic structure with the idea that it was an impossible task. In most of my youth I avoided this mountain, trying to replace its space in my life with a more pleasant, accessible object. This mountain, my unlearned parents kept drilling into my head, "Once you have climbed the mountain, the quicker you will see a new world," a world with new ideas and new roads that would give new serenity, that no language can describe. They often told me of how they had desired to climb the mountains in their lifetimes, but had never been given an opportunity to make the pilgrimage upward.

After my hitch in the army I took another look at my mountain, but it had not diminished one iota. I swiftly turned away to keep from facing a job that was inevitable. I got married and was raising a family when I got the urge like never before to climb my mountain. Knowing what was involved I began to climb the rough side of the mountain for the past 20 years, but now I am glad for my journey. Everyday get sweeter than the day before. My sweat and tears have turned into joy, my experiences into knowledge.

I am now postulating as my parents did before me that everyone should start early in life climbing his or her mountain. No one else can make the journey for you. Every child and every adult must climb his own mountain. I have only one regret, I should have started my excursion safari earlier in my life. Now I really understand what the Apostle Paul meant, "All things worketh together for good to them that love the Lord."

Please keep in mind that Bishop Thompson wrote this as a young man, in psychological terms. He continues:

My mountain was the obstacle that I was to encounter in life. Once I had reached the peak of the mountain requiring the knowledge and experiences of life, I would find peace.

THE PRINCIPLE OF FAITH

Jesus says, "I came that you may have life, and that you may have it more abundantly." I also love what Jesus says to us in the gospels:

And Jesus said unto them, Because of your unbelief: for verily I say unto you, If ye have faith as a grain of mustard seed, ye shall say unto this mountain, Remove hence to yonder place; and it shall remove; and nothing shall be impossible unto you.
(Matthew 17:20)

Jesus answered and said unto them, Verily, I say unto you, If ye have faith, and doubt not, ye shall not only do this which is done to the fig tree, but also if ye shall say unto this mountain, Be thou removed, and be thou cast into the sea; it shall be done. And all things, whatsoever ye shall ask in prayer, believing, ye shall receive.
(Matthew 21:21-22)

Here we have two different situations where Jesus more or less asks us to apply the same principle, the principle of faith. My husband had faith that one day his vision would become a reality. "It will come, it will not tarry."

In keeping with the vision God imparted in him through the person of the Holy Spirit, it was time for another birth. September 10, 1979 at 10:00am, Truth Evangelistic Temple Christian Academy opened its doors, with Dr. James Oliver Thompson as Principal. The staff, including volunteers, was in place to welcome approximately 50 students. The vision "Evangelism through Education" had become a reality, with the goal of reaching the community and surrounding areas one child at a time. The aim was to train and educate children and youth of all ages intellectually, physically, socially, emotionally and spiritually, using biblically-based curriculum.

Bishop vowed that no student should be deprived of an education. He remained focused on this purpose as he reminded me, "It was not easy." He believed in the vision that God gave him, and he also believed that God would bring it into existence.

DEFYING ALL ODDS

At this point, I need to say that we cannot separate the man from his vision, which is an integral part of him. There was opposition when he shared with some people about opening a Christian school. Some said that it could not be done, while others were flat against it. I am reminded of Nehemiah when he wanted to rebuild the walls of Jerusalem.

And I arose in the night, I and some few men with me; neither told I any man what my God had put in my heart to do at Jerusalem. Neither was there any beast with me, save the beast that I rode upon.
(Nehemiah 2:12)

Nehemiah had Sanballat and Tobiah, who opposed the very thing that God had put in his heart to do.

Defying all odds, my husband strove to keep the momentum alive. After a few years of toiling and getting into position, it was time for the first graduating class of 1983. The following are actual excerpts from the speech which Dr. James Thompson gave in his own words.

Praise the Lord, and congratulations class of 1983 on your magnificent achievement; you are now the first graduates of Truth Evangelistic Temple Christian Academy (TET Christian Academy). You are also the first alumni class, which makes your achievement worthy of double honor. So we say, "Praise the Lord" again. This occasion marks a milestone in my life, seeing that I waited 20 years to see a dream come to pass. God told me He was going to start a Christian school through the ministry that He gave to me, and He brought it into reality. "For they that wait upon the Lord shall renew their strength, they shall mount up with wings as eagles; they shall run, and not be weary; and they shall walk, and not faint."

Yes, I admit it has been a long and tedious journey. I got tired on the way, but I thank God, like many of you graduates, I did not get tired of the way.

To the parents, I would like to give special thanks. You were brave and courageous, and you demonstrated those

37

qualities as you stood by the school. You are an outstanding and unique group of parents and to you I offer a big round of applause. TET Christian Academy has been blessed to have students and parents such as you to be the progenitors of a great institute of learning.

To our untouchable staff, I praise you for the magnificent, yet unbelievable job that you have done in these past four years. You too have stood to tell in an outstanding way; you have been faithful, sincere, brave and plain hardworking since the inauguration of TET.

Graduates, you are the pioneers of yesterday, and you are the pioneers of tomorrow concerning Christian education. You have and still are awaiting your names on the pages of history.

May God bless you and all yours in Christ (Pastor James Thompson, PhD).

"Addressing the first graduating class of TET was one my proudest moments," he said to me, while stressing the face that this was God's promise that He had given him through the vision he had received as a young man, 28 years old.

The Vision

The prophet Joel said, "Young men will see visions, old men will dream dreams." Bishop saw the vision as a young man, and then started to have dreams of seeing this vision come to pass.

This is what he wrote concerning "his meadow and its interpretation."

Physiologically speaking, my meadow is spherical in composition. It has a long path that leadeth to the entrance. At the beginning of the entrance, there are many caves and rocks in the ground. The closer you get to the entrance of the path it begins to smooth out, and the pitfalls, caves and rocks seem to dispatch. As I pass the entrance there seems to be thousand of impulses drawing at the faculties of the body, especially the control tower which is my mind.

Each time I enter my meadow, I begin to reminisce. At first sight, all of the paths, rocks, streams and the little valleys were strange, dissonant and unharmonious. As I began to dwell in the midst of these unrelated figures and pictures, there seemed to be a togetherness. My mind became so ecstatic at the great revelation these revealed. Although they seemed so dissonant and unharmonious they were working together to demonstrate a common cause and perspective. Out of this hidden darkness of disorganization came understanding and knowledge. This experience cannot be found without peace and serenity from within one's own self.

My meadow brings things together and gives them understanding in my life. It helps me to realize that all things work together for good to them that love the Lord.

The Apostle Paul left us with this full assurance from God. *"Being confident of this very thing, that he which hath begun a good work in you will perform it until the day of Jesus Christ"* (Philippians 1:6). Our minds may go through psychological thinking; however, we must be in control of its contents in order to bring into perspective those things that God is revealing to us.

CHAPTER SIX

A New Milestone

Whoso findeth a wife findeth a good thing, and obtaineth favour of the Lord.

(Proverbs 18:22)

THROUGH THICK AND THIN

This was one of my husband's favorite Scriptures. He would say to me, "And I've found a good thing, the Lord has blessed me to have two good wives."

As we conversed as usual, he spoke about his late wife Henrietta, on whom he was dependent to reach out in her special way. He was also a family-oriented and conscientious person who loved his children and other relatives. He told me about his only daughter, and her love for gadgets, like his. I observed a half-grin on his face when he said, "She stayed with me through thick and thin." He then gave a chuckle and said, "None of my boys seems to want to follow in my footsteps."

At times the naps are at more frequent intervals, but he would defend himself by saying, "All shuteye is not sleep, all good-byes are not gone."

When we met, it was four days after St. Valentine's Day, 1999. I was getting ready to attend noonday prayer. When the husky voice on the other end of the phone spoke to me, I was stalling for time. I wanted to get my hair done. He in turn would not take "no" for an answer. We met right after noonday prayer that Thursday. He was very jovial and talkative, had a big grin on his face. He stood around 5'6", though he looked somewhat shorter to me.

When we met, there was a tie that bound us together. Two lives were propelled together by the Holy Ghost. I learned when we met that he was very faithful to the church, and to God's people.

SOMETHING ABOUT THAT ROOM

Six years later as we sat in the living room, where we always sit together and communicate, things began to unfold. There is something about that room. This is his writing, "My Room," and its interpretation:

I sit in my living room which is on the first floor in my home. It is a large, spacious room about 20 feet long and about 15 feet wide. The walls are impaneled a cream white, the ceiling paint is old and peeling off the walls.

Sometimes I sit and reminisce. While meditating I see my body deteriorating, but I thank God for picking up the pieces.

42

Beside each of the two windows, there are radiators to keep the room warm and pleasant. I really sink into a state of unconsciousness in a sense, and let my thoughts drift gloriously into space without walls. There my mind is able to feel the presence of something that is strange, but comforting to my mind. The room itself is not captivating, or even attractive, but there is a sense of completeness, of wholeness, of reaching the goal about the dwelling. The room has not been decorated for visitors, but completely for me. I appreciate its beauty; it is mine. I created it with my own two hands according to my wishes. The floor is hard without covering, but is spotless. Oh! There is a piano in the room, but unfortunately, I do not play any musical instruments.

This next portion he entitles "The Analysis of My Room":

In my analysis there will be no picture or statuesque symbols, because my background is from the ghetto. Everything was basic; the only thing fancy about my environment was the fantasies and the daydreams. The spacious room does not represent a life of emptiness, but of peace and tranquility. The old paint peeling off the wall is not a life that has begun to deteriorate or has began to disintegrate, but a life of simplicity, one of plainness. It is not normality, but the windows are my perspective and concept of the life's span which I have traveled. It is this input from the windows, electrified by the radiators, which generates comfort throughout my body and soul. My room is a system where my years of experiences are stored. It is filled with positives, negatives, triumphs and failures, but all encounters are translated into completeness.

My room can be nicknamed "The room of experience." It is by this storehouse I can face and deal with the magnitudes of positives, negatives, triumphs and failures which I encountered in my life, whose progenitor is the neo-society. There is always an...answer in my storehouse for the new encounter.

In his description of the living room, I had the opportunity of spending the last six years in sharing the tranquility, and the sense of completeness. It's not really your typical living room, with all the fine furniture, and well-decorated features. The room has been made smaller; however, it was still his domain. His special spot included: his chair, table, along with his laptop computer, Bible, spelling notebook, and don't forget, his gadgets. We also had moments of intense discussions on the Bible, family, friends, the church, school and things of a personal nature. I had to remind him at times about his office upstairs. From 1978, nothing changed much. Getting up early in the morning was one of his common practices, "I have to open the doors of the school." He was a very timely person, very strict, especially when it came to the church and school. Each time I looked at him as he got weaker, his determination was still to do what he had been doing for the past 39 years. He had "A charge to keep." He kept it diligently and faithfully.

CHAPTER SEVEN

Passing the Torch

One of the proudest moments of my life spent with my husband, was when he was consecrated a Bishop. I sensed this peace coming from within him. In May of 2005 when I saw him standing before the altar, being robed, the anointing of God rested upon him. He had a special glow that only God alone could give. He was always addressed as "Bishop" even before the consecration service.

During these moments, there were bouts of difficulties with his breathing. At times it looked as if he were about to draw his last breath. His armor bearer, one of the Elders, was very instrumental in assisting him throughout the Scriptures. My husband's motto was, "I have to live right," and that he did without any question. At times the enemy would play with my mind, even throughout service, trying to get me to think negative thoughts. My thoughts went back to the Apostle Paul and his writing concerning Christian virtues.

We as Christians should keep our thoughts occupied with:

...whatsoever things are true, whatsoever things are honest, whatsoever things are just, whatsoever things are pure whatsoever things are lovely, whatsoever things are of good report; if there be any virtue, and if there be any praise, think on these things.

(Philippians 4:8)

I began to realize that seeing my husband standing before the altar with God's anointing being manifested; that was true, honest, pure, lovely, and of good report. He told me that some people thought that he waited too long to be consecrated as Bishop. He would say to me:

I have planted, Apollos watered; but God gave the increase. So then neither is he that planteth any thing, neither he that watereth; but God that giveth the increase.

(1 Corinthians 3:6-7)

He was not in a hurry according to man's timing.

I SHALL NOT DIE, BUT LIVE

As time moved on, my husband grew somewhat weaker, where he panted for breath with each movement; he got to the point where he did not want to exert himself. One Sunday morning during his sermon, he informed the church that in case of his demise one of his elders would be the pastor. During our conversation at home, he would drop little hints here and there concerning death.

46

It is very pertinent to know that even through his weaknesses and disabilities, the "vision" was still very first and foremost in his mind. At times he could not make it to the school; he would call the teachers to find out if everything was going well. He would also try to hide his true feelings of how he felt physically from me. But I could detect his pain. He would oftentimes quote this Scripture:

I shall not die, but live, and declare the works of the Lord. The Lord hath chastened me sore; but He hath not given me over unto death.
(Psalm 118:17-18)

At this point he was mostly concerned that he not die spiritually. He looked at me with a stare one evening, then asked me this question, "Sweetie, did anyone ever prophesy to you that you were going to be a widow?" I was not prepared for this. I managed to say, "Please don't talk like that."

A STUDENT OF PSYCHOLOGY

This is another excerpt from his writing: "My Chapel and Its Interpretation."

My chapel does not sit on the hill, neither does it sit in the valley. It is not seen by other human eyes, in fact I do not see it with my own human perception; I simply know it is there with beauty and tranquility. Human hands do not feel it, but it is so tangible I can feel its contents all over me. While I am there I am elevated to a high plain that enables me to reminisce and look down on the environment and its constituencies. There is such beauty that has never been

47

able to be visualized with human eyes. Without the aid of such a vehicle as the eye, I can still see my loved ones, and those who surround me without prejudice, without influence of my ego and superego. I can see them without the cravings of my id. I see them all standing in the green Garden of Eden without any human influence or spiritual wickedness, with nothing but what God had in them back in that Garden when they became living souls. It is in this chapel that I see men for what they are like, without the prejudice of this world influencing my perspective.

"THE ANALYSIS OF MY CHAPEL"

My chapel is like the pre-rapture of the true Church of God. "Then we which are alive and remain shall be caught up together with them in the cloud to meet the Lord in the air and so shall we ever be with the Lord." When entering my chapel it is like being raptured up to be in the presence of Christ. I forget those things that are around me. I forget those things that are transpired. I am stripped of my human sagacity, stripped of my mortal body. Sometimes my closeness to the supreme becomes so evolved that there are times when I can say as the Apostle Paul, "Whether in the body or not I do not know," but inner tranquility and serenity are flowing in my soul. It is in my chapel that I see men for what they are and the real world as it really is, as an inhabitant. But I also see the righteous world, and men for what they are.

In conclusion, my chapel is my spiritual self, my inner desires. Once I am outside my chapel there again the conflict begins, because I interact with the world and men. I am learning to enter in my chapel at many locations. Therefore I am able to find a great deal more tranquility as I grow older than when I was younger.

My husband, in his writings, used some psychoanalytic terms. In all of this, he was very conscious of God and His divine presence. I am also a student of psychology; I understand the Freudian's Theories very clearly, however, the best theory is the theory of Jesus Christ. Here is some of Freud's Theory of Personality; as I understand it to be:

Id:
The most primitive part of personality which remains unconscious, supplies energy to other parts of the psyche, and demands immediate gratification.

Pleasure principle:
The principle under which the id operates, consisting of a desire for immediate satisfaction of wishes, desires or needs.

Psyche:
The mind, mental life, and personality as a whole

Executive Ego:
The executive portion of personality in Freudian theory charged with directing rational, realistic behavior.

Superego:
An internalization of parental values and societal standards.

Conscience:
The part of the superego that causes guilt when its standards are not met.[1]

APPROVED BY GOD

We as born-again believers know that the Holy Spirit is our guide and connection to God. We believe that the Word of God is our source to our spiritual, physical, and mental healing. My husband writes about his chapel, where he views things in the spirit.

In choosing his successor, my husband approached God for His approval. He would say to me, "Sweetie, I want to make sure that I do the right thing." Moses and Joshua came to my mind:

And the Lord said unto Moses, Behold thy days approach that thou must die: call Joshua, and present yourselves in the tabernacle of the congregation, that I may give him a charge. And Moses and Joshua went, and presented themselves in the tabernacle, of the congregation.
(Deuteronomy 31:14)

I had the opportunity to be an eyewitness to God's servant, a leader who loved Him with all his heart, who consulted Him. He was comfortable with the choice which God gave him to be the pastor. The Psalmist David leaves us this instruction,

Except the Lord build the house, they labor in vain that build it: except the Lord keep the city, the watchmen waketh but in vain.
(Psalm 127:1)

HEALED BY GOD

Bishop Thompson's writings:

I decided to attend church one Sunday morning with my wife (his late wife Henrietta) *who was a faithful member of the church. At this time of my life* (28 years old) *I had drifted away from the teachings of the church. I sat noticing the different things that were taking place during the service. I became captivated by some unexplainable feelings, which occupied all of my attention. One of the great phenomena of the black church is the manifestation of the Holy Spirit amongst the parishioners. When the preacher began to do an exegesis of the Scriptures my soul began to feel uplifted. His simple, but captivating, message touched my intellect. I was persuaded to give my heart to God.*

Since that time I have been active in the church and working for the purpose of God, which is to get people saved and into the church. One of my recent spiritual experiences would be how God healed my body (he was 47 years old at the time of his healing) *from an infection that I suffered in my leg.*

I am reiterating the customs of the black church, for they are very different from the white church's customs. Blacks learned to depend upon and have faith in God many years before things became so prosperous and they were able to visit the doctors.

My infection seemed to have reached the worst condition. In previous times I did most of the baptizing at my church, but with the new ministers coming in, I slowed down some, and let them do the baptizing.

51

This Sunday morning, four souls gave their hearts to the Lord; the custom in the Apostolic church is to baptize them that very hour. The Lord spoke to me and told to do the baptizing. We usually wear boots in the pool, however, this special Sunday, I was told by the Holy Ghost not to wear the boots. Just before I stepped down into the clear blue water, I prayed the prayer of faith, "Lord, trouble the water as you did for the men at the pool of Bethesda."

I baptized the four candidates; while I was in the water I felt a transformation taking place in my leg. As I was experiencing the phenomena, I believed God. When I came out of the water my leg was completely healed. From that day to this I have never been back to the doctor for any sickness; God has kept my body healed for five years. I do believe in doctors, and the fine jobs that they are doing, and have done in the past. It is a true fact that the Lord speaks to believers, and when He does, truth will always be seen in its fullness. As St. Ambrose says, "Let Thy good spirit enter my heart and there be heard without utterance, and without the sound of works speak all truth."

All believers should listen to the voice of the Spirit; in order to know and identify His voice, one must have a relationship with God. This relationship should be an intimate one. Jesus said, "My sheep know My voice, and a stranger they will not follow." God desires to have that special oneness with His believers.

Chapter Eight

The Last Mile

For I am now ready to be offered, and the time of my departure is at hand. I have fought a good fight, I have finished my course, I have kept the faith: henceforth there is laid up for me a crown of righteousness, which the Lord, the righteous judge, shall give me at that day: and not to me only, but unto all them also that love His appearing.

(2 Timothy 4:6-8)

Staying on Course

The wonderful words of the Apostle Paul are so appropriate and well-deserved, and applicable to Bishop James Thompson's lifestyle. He fought with internal and external conflicts throughout his life, yet his belief and faith in God kept him on a course which impacted every area of his accomplishments. The Apostle Paul points out that "a crown of righteousness" is laid up for him, but not only for him, it is for all of us who love His appearing.

We as believers are in a champion fight, wrestling with Satan and his demonic forces; in this fight, we have to depend on the Holy Spirit's empowerment which enables us to defeat Satan.

Departure at Hand

I really do believe that God imparted to my husband that his departure was at hand.

Somewhere around 2002-2003, I learned from the doctor that my husband was seriously ill. My prayer life became more enhanced, wherein I now had to fast more while approaching God on my husband's behalf. The thought of "kidney failure" ran a chill through my body, seeing that I have knowledge concerning medical problems. He, in turn, was never too ill to pray; he had difficulty getting on his knees, but managed to get there somehow. At times I heard him say, "Lord, I have done my best, I hope that You are pleased with me." As I watched him, the pain of his sufferings was being felt within me. I also sensed in my spirit the prayers of the saints.

In 2005, his condition grew worse; he refused to have the dialysis which the doctor suggested; he was believing God for healing. We started to miss service at different times as his breathing problems became more intense. My mind went back to when we had celebrated his seventieth birthday, when the Spirit of the Lord brought this Scripture to my spirit:

> *Because he hath set his love upon Me, therefore will I deliver him: I will set him on high, because he hath*

*known My name. He shall call upon Me, and I will
answer him: I will be with him in trouble; I will
deliver him, and honour him. With long life will I
satisfy him, and shew him My salvation.*

(Psalm 91:14-16)

DWELLING IN THE SECRET PLACE

When the Spirit of God birthed these Scripture verses in
me, I began to dwell on this, "With long life will I satisfy him,
and shew him My salvation." Once I started to trust God to
bring this to pass, the enemy bombarded my mind, then my
husband's condition began to worsen; it was like everything
that could have gone wrong, went wrong. I turned my heart
to the beginning of Psalm 91:

*He that dwelleth in the secret place of the most High
shall abide under the shadow of the Almighty. I will
say of the Lord, He is my refuge and my fortress: my
God; in Him will I trust.*

(Psalm 91:1-2)

This became a reality in my life from then until now; I
realized that:

First: I have to <u>dwell</u> in the secret place.
Second: The "secret place" <u>belongs to God</u>.
Third: <u>God's shadow covers me</u>.
Fourth: I had to make <u>a confession</u>:
Fifth: God, You are <u>my refuge</u>, and <u>my fortress</u>
Sixth: Since You are <u>my God, I trust You, I am
           depending on You</u>.

With this in my mind, things began to get more enlightened; the Word of God became alive in me, more than ever.

FOCUSING ON THE VISION

On December 12, 2005, a Monday to be precise, my husband was ready to go down to the school. We had moved our bed down to the living room area, while the living room went upstairs. He sat up in his chair as usual, and then got on the phone, where he called up a few of his old members from the church who were in different states. His mood was happy; he managed to chuckle some. I was in my favorite chair and overheard some of the conversations; they were about the good old days at Truth Evangelistic Temple (TET) church. He was still focusing on the "vision."

December 13, 2005, I noticed that his breathing was very labored. He was extremely weak, but refused to let me call the ambulance or have someone come to take us to the doctors. He read his Bible, prayed and continued to be concerned with the church and the school. At times in the night he sat on the side of the bed; there was oxygen in the house, which he used constantly. The Nebulizer machine could be heard every four hours or less.

On December 14, 2005, he could hardly get out of his bed; he insisted that he wanted to sit in his chair. I assisted him to the chair, then this is what he said to me, "Sweetie, please sit right there in your chair, where I can get a good look at you." I became very puzzled, and some funny sensations began to emerge from within me. At one point, after he went into one of his long naps, I managed to tip toe to the kitchen. I heard his voice, which became so weak, saying, "Sweetie, where are you?" I immediately rushed back to the chair. He then started winking both eyes at me. Then some gestured kisses. As I sat there, I watched him go in and out of naps, with a spirit of contentment.

Later on that very evening, he opened his eyes, then he said to me, "Bring my coat, rest it on the bed. Bring your coat, rest it on the bed. Then sweetie, sit down, I have to talk to you. After I am finished talking to you, call the two elders, at the church, and my daughter also. Then call 911."

We had the TV on the Music Choice Gospel station for the day. Just then I heard this song and managed to get a few of the lines, which goes something like this:

When you don't hear My voice, please follow My plans, I am preparing you for Myself.

I heard the voice of the Holy Spirit, promptings on the inside, saying: "I am preparing you for what is about to happen.". I became emotional, and the tears were flowing, when my husband's voice was heard saying: "Sweetie, don't cry, I am going to be alright."

"…you are going to be alright." He managed to repeat this twice.

After he finished talking to me, I called 911. They were at the house between five and six minutes later. He was still conscious; all he would say is, "I can't breathe."

In August of this same year we had gone to Lancaster, PA, for a vacation where he had an episode of Dysphea (painful breathing). I had to call 911; he was hospitalized. After we got home, he told me that this was our last vacation.

I AM WHO GOD SAYS I AM

When the ambulance came, we were off to the hospital. When he said to me, "Sweetie, I can't breathe," the memories of that ordeal lingered in my mind. I was helpless, even with the medications that gave temporary relief and our prayers; yet I had to be strong for him.

I rode in the front of the ambulance; it seemed to me that it was not in much of a hurry. When we arrived at the hospital, they whisked my husband to the emergency room, and then asked the family to stay in the waiting room.

While in the waiting room, it was if my mind was playing a movie of our life together. It went from the time we met in 1999 until that night in the hospital waiting room. Our life story played out in my mind.

The Holy Spirit comforted me, then when I saw someone coming to the waiting room, my belly began to burn. She pushed open the door and asked for Mrs. Thompson. I knew that the news was bad. She told me that his heart had stopped, and that they had tried to revive him around five times, but failed.

Later on, they asked if I wanted to look at him. The Elder and I went in, where I looked at his lifeless body. He looked like someone at peace. On the other hand, I was in a place where I could not believe that my husband was gone.

After I came home from the hospital, I noticed on his pad where he had written:

> "I am who God says I am.
> I can do what God says I can do."

He had managed to experience the full manifestation of the vision given to him by God, which he faithful expedited truthfully and passionately. His vision now lives on.

CHAPTER NINE

Sermons by Bishop James Thompson, PhD

- Submission of the Wife
- I was Influenced
- Teachings on Consecration
- Children of Adoption

SUBMISSION OF THE WIFE

The Holy Spirit makes communion with God possible, and we are controlled by the Spirit. This makes it a vital sin for man or woman not to obey the Spirit. *"Quench not the Spirit"* (1 Thessalonians 5:19).

There is only one statement about marriage that God makes four times in the Bible.

> *For this cause shall a man leave his father and mother and cleave to his wife, and they twain shall become one flesh.*
> (Genesis 2:24, Matthew 19:5, Mark 10:7-8, and Ephesians 5:31)

The husband and wife must submit to one another, and they should have humility toward one another.

> *Submitting yourselves to one another in the fear of God.*
> (Ephesians 5:21)

When we look at Ephesians 5:22-6:4, we see the relationship of all the parties that are involved in a family relationship: the wife, the husband, and the children. They are supposed to emphasize submission.

Submission is not merely a concept for women. It is a principle for all Bible believers.

> *Let nothing be done through strife or vainglory; but in lowliness of mind let each esteem other better than themselves. Look not on his own things, but every man also on the things of others.*
> (Philippians 2:3-4)

Likewise, ye younger, submit yourselves to the elder. Yea, all of you be subject one to another, and be clothed with humility: for God resisteth the proud, and giveth grace to the humble.

(1 Peter 5:5)

Let every soul be subject unto the higher powers. For there is no power but of God: the powers that be are ordained of God.

(Romans 13:1)

Obey them that have the rule over you, and submit yourselves: for they watch for your souls, as they that must give account, that they may do it with joy, and not with grief: for that is unprofitable for you.

(Hebrews 13:17)

Submission does not mean that the wife never opens her mouth.

She openeth her mouth with wisdom; and in her tongue is the law of kindness.

(Proverbs 31:26)

And he began to speak boldly in the synagogue: whom when Aquila and Priscilla had heard, they took him unto them, and expounded unto him the way of God more perfectly.

(Acts 18:26)

But the angel of the LORD did no more appear to Manoah and to his wife. Then Manoah knew that he was an angel of the LORD. And Manoah said unto his wife, We shall surely die, because we have seen God. But his wife said unto him, If the LORD were pleased to kill us, he would not have received a burnt offering and a meat offering at

61

*our hands, neither would he have shewed us all
these things, nor would as at this time have told
us such things as these .*

(Judges 13:21-23)

**Submission does not mean that the wife becomes
a wallflower** who folds up and allows her abilities to lie
dormant.

*Who can find a virtuous woman? for her price is
far above rubies. The heart of her husband doth
safely trust in her, so that he shall have no need
of spoil. She will do him good and not evil all the
days of her life.*

(Proverbs 31:10-12)

*She layeth her hands to the spindle, and her hands
hold the distaff. She stretcheth out her hand to the
poor; yea, she reacheth forth her hands to the needy.
She is not afraid of the snow for her household: for
all her household are clothed with scarlet. Strength
and honour are her clothing; and she shall rejoice in
time to come. She looketh well to the ways of her
household, and eateth not the bread of idleness. Her
children arise up, and call her blessed; her husband
also, and he praiseth her. Give her of the fruit of her
hands; and let her own works praise her in the
gates.*

(Proverbs 31:19-21, 25, 27-28, 31)

**Subjection does not mean that the wife is inferior
to the husband.**

Jesus Christ was not inferior to Mary and Joseph, but
listen to what Luke says:

And he said unto them, How is it that ye sought me? wist ye not that I must be about my Father's business? And they understood not the saying which he spake unto them. And he went down with them, and came to Nazareth, and was subject unto them: but his mother kept all these sayings in her heart. And Jesus increased in wisdom and stature, and in favour with God and man.

(Luke 2:49-52)

Jesus was in no way inferior to God; for Christ was and is fully and completely God. *"I and My Father are One"* (John 10:30). Yet we hear Jesus saying:

I can of Mine own self do nothing: as I hear, I judge: and My judgment is just; because I seek not Mine own will, but the will of the Father which hath sent Me.

(John 5:30)

So now we understand that submission of the wife does not in any way signify that woman is inferior to man. But that submission is God's order and structure of teaching responsibility within the home.

And God said, Let us make man in Our image, after Our likeness: and let them have dominion over the fish of the sea, and over the fowl of the air, and over the cattle, and over all the earth, and over every creeping thing that creepeth upon the earth. So God created man in His own image, in the image of God created He him; male and female created He them.

(Genesis 1:26-27)

And Adam said, This is now bone of my bones, and flesh of my flesh: she shall be called Woman, because she was taken out of Man.

(Genesis 2:23)

There is neither Jew nor Greek, there is neither bond nor free, there is neither male nor female: for ye are all one in Christ Jesus.

(Galatians 3:28)

What has been said thus far asserts the equalitarian status and dignity of women and men.

I WAS INFLUENCED

Influence! What does this word really express, and what is the message that is being conveyed? The dictionary gives the meaning of influence as to affect or altar by influence: to have an effect on, or development; the act or power of producing an effect without apparent force or direct authority; the power or capacity of causing an effect in an indirect or intangible way.

The kind of lifestyle a person has, why he is behaving in a particular way, his likes and dislikes, what caused him to choose the vocation that he did are all a matter of influence. What causes him to buy the type of clothes he wears? Why did he buy one type of car instead of a different kind? What motivated him to strive to reach goals that seem far out of reach? The age-old question comes to one's mind: why? This same question often comes to one's mind, even if a person is successful. The answer is always the same: **influence**. In many of theses instances it was advertising that one saw on TV or a billboard, etc.

I remember when I was growing up as a boy. I was so influenced by one of my classmates and his family that I wished many times that I could be in that family. That desire built a hunger within me to achieve, to try to be somebody great in life. Like many other young men, when my dreams turned out to be nothing but a mirage in the desert, I took to the bottle, which led me to a downward path. But I thank God for Jesus who gave me a glorious and abundant life that could not be found in my friends or any of my peers. So it is a real fact that influence has had a great part in shaping people's lives. The Bible gives a good outline concerning influence in the first Psalm.

BLESSED (HAPPY, fortunate, prosperous, and enviable) is the man who walks and lives not in the counsel of the ungodly [following their advice, their plans and purposes], nor stands [submissive and inactive] in the path where sinners walk, nor sits down [to relax and rest] where the scornful [and the mockers] gather. But his delight and desire are in the law of the Lord, and on His law (the precepts, the instructions, the teachings of God) he habitually meditates (ponders and studies) by day and by night. And he shall be like a tree firmly planted [and tended] by the streams of water, ready to bring forth its fruit in its season; its leaf also shall not fade or wither; and everything he does shall prosper [and come to maturity].

(Psalm 1:1-3, AMP)

But let us take a look at the second man's influence and his lifestyle.

Not so the wicked [those disobedient and living without God are not so]. But they are like the chaff [worthless, dead, without substance] which the wind drives away. Therefore the wicked [those disobedient and living without God] shall not stand [justified] in the judgment, nor sinners in the congregation of the righteous [those who are upright and in right standing with God]. For the Lord knows and is fully acquainted with the way of the righteous, but the way of the ungodly [those living outside God's will] shall perish (end in ruin and come to nought).

(Psalm 1:4-6, AMP)

What is the real makeup of a godly man? In Genesis we are told:

And God said, Let us make man in Our image, after Our likeness: and let them have dominion over the fish of the sea, and over the fowl of the air, and over the cattle, and over all the earth.

(Genesis 1:26)

It can be emphatically seen here that the godly man is not a creature to be influenced, but is to influence. He has a mandate from God to rule, control and influence the whole world. This glorious, beautiful world that God made is in the hands of the godly man to preserve its lifestyle, according to God's criteria. The godly man is the salt of the earth and is responsible to permeate the world with a theocracy system.

But the ungodly man and his evil influence is working hard to overthrow this godly system, and replace it with humanism. God is a triune being. He presents Himself as Father in creation, Son in redemption, and Holy Ghost acting upon creation in this dispensation of grace. But He is still one God. So man, being made in the image of God, is body, soul, and spirit.

> *And the very God of peace sanctify you wholly; and I pray God your whole spirit and soul and body be preserved blameless unto the coming of our Lord Jesus Christ.*
> (1 Thessalonians 5:23)

There must be a divine unity in the tri-unity of God. Of course, what other kind could there be possible in the God-head?

> *Howbeit when He, the Spirit of truth, is come, He will guide you into all truth: for He shall not speak of Himself; but whatsoever He shall hear, that shall He speak: and He will shew you things to come. He shall glorify Me: for He shall receive of Mine, and shall shew it unto you. All things that the Father hath are Mine: therefore said I, that He shall take of Mine, and shall shew it unto you.*
> (John 16:13-15)

This same kind of unity must be actively engaged, functioning and cooperating in that glorious body of Christ (the Church) at all times. It will take this kind of example if the world is going to be influenced to follow in the steps of the godly man. For the footsteps of a godly man are ordered by God.

It does appear in this Scripture that there is no joy in living the lifestyle of the ungodly. Why, then, would anyone want to leave the best for second best? Who would want to leave a home of plenty, to go live and eat with the swine? (Prodigal son) The ungodly have no stability, no anchorage. He is worthless. He is worldly, he is sensual, and he has no hope, for he is driven by every wind and doctrine.

If we who are [abiding] in Christ have hope only in this life and that is all, then we are of all people most miserable and to be pitied.
(1 Corinthians 15:19, AMP)

We are living in a world of miserable people, in many different categories and degrees. Many of them who know Christ are miserable because of a wrong view of Him; they have no hope beyond this life. Others are miserable because they never knew Him in the first place.

If the saints of God have hope only in this present world, then all the teaching of the Bible concerning the hope of life after death is a cruel mistake. God has created appetites which He cannot satisfy, He has excited hopes which must perish in death, and if our hopes perish in death, then neither Jesus nor the saints have victory over death, Hell and the grave. God has built a great ship and must destroy it because He cannot create a sea in which it can float. Jesus has died in vain.

Oh! Only a fool could believe lies such as this one. Only a fool could think of a Mighty God such as ours that would fool His children and break a divine promise which He has made by His dear Son.

Let not your heart be troubled: ye believe in God, believe also in Me. In My Father's house are many mansions: if it were not so, I would have told you. I go to prepare a place for you. And if I go and pre-

pare a place for you, I will come again, and receive you unto Myself; that where I am, there ye may be also.

(John 14:1-3)

The ungodly man is always anxious to try and influence the child of God by giving his worldly advice and counseling. Eve was not on the devil's ground, she was in the Garden where God had placed her, but the devil came into the Garden to influence her. The saints can thank God for the blood of Jesus that was shed on Calvary cross, so when old Satan comes on the saint's ground, he can plead the blood of Christ.

This also serves the saints notice never to go on the devil's territory. Where is his territory? The movies, dances, swimming half naked in public pools – any ungodly place where Christ cannot be glorified.

How did the devil trick Eve? He did it with false counsel. He told her that God did not want her to eat of the tree of good and evil because they would become gods. It is such a sad thing for a person to let another person come into the church and influence them to leave the church and go serve the devil who has already been condemned to hell with his angels.

YOU poor and silly and thoughtless and unreflecting and senseless Galatians! Who has fascinated or bewitched or cast a spell over you, unto whom—right before your very eyes—Jesus Christ (the Messiah) was openly and graphically set forth and portrayed as crucified? Let me ask you this one question: Did you receive the [Holy] Spirit as the result of obeying the Law and doing its

69

works, or was it by hearing [the message of the Gospel] and believing [it]? [Was it from observing a law of rituals or from a message of faith?] Are you so foolish and so senseless and so silly? Having begun [your new life spiritually] with the [Holy] Spirit, are you now reaching perfection [by dependence] on the flesh?

(Galatians 3:1-3, AMP)

When we consider the influence of the ungodly upon our present society, surely all must agree there is a great need for godly men who are full of truth and righteousness. Godly men need to take back the government of the nation, take back the public schools, take back the children from the influence of liberalism. The ungodly are baiting their influence with pleasure, unreal pleasure that is catching the eyes of the youth in America.

Do You Remember the Real America?

By American Educational League

Do You Remember when riots were unthinkable?

Do You Remember when you left your front doors open?

Do You Remember when socialism was a dirty word?

Do You Remember when the flag was a sacred symbol?

Do You Remember when criminals actually went to jail?

Do You Remember when you weren't afraid to go out at night?

Do You Remember when taxes were only a necessary nuisance?

Do You Remember when a boy was a boy, and dressed like one?

Do You Remember when a girl was a girl and dressed like one?

Do You Remember when the clergy actually talked about religion?

Do You Remember when clerks and repairmen tried to please you?

Do You Remember when college kids swallowed goldfish, not acid?

Do You Remember when young fellows tried to join the Army or Navy?

Do You Remember when you knew what the Fourth of July stood for?

Do You Remember when you never dreamed our country could ever lose?

Do You Remember when you bragged about our hometown and home state?

Do You Remember when you weren't embarrassed to say that this is the best country in the world?

Do You Remember when America was a land filled with brave, proud, confident, hardworking people?

Enter not into the path of the wicked, and go not in the way of evil men. Avoid it, pass not by it, turn from it, and pass away. For they sleep not, except they have done mischief; and their sleep is taken away, unless they cause some to fall. For they eat the bread of wickedness, and drink the wine of violence. But the path of the just is as the shining light, that shineth more and more unto the perfect day. The way of the wicked is as darkness: they know not at what they stumble. My son, attend to my words; incline thine ear unto my sayings.

(Proverbs 4:14-20)

TEACHINGS ON CONSECRATION

Introduction:

The word "consecration" in the Old Testament means "devote, separate, set apart for the service of glory of God."

The word occurs twice in the New Testament.

For the law maketh men high priests which have infirmity; but the word of the oath which was since the law [maketh] the Son, who is consecrated for evermore.

(Hebrews 7:28)

By a new and living way, which He hath consecrated for us, through the veil, that is to say, His flesh.

(Hebrews 10:20)

- Consecration does not mean conversion or a state of sinless perfection.

- Consecration is not necessarily a sudden impulse or emotion developed in excitement.

- Consecration is simply the soul trusting wholly in Jesus, no holding back in reserve.

It is giving ourselves up to Christ forever as bought with a price, no longer our own. It is not necessarily volunteering for full time service, though that might develop.

> *The gold for things of gold, and the silver for things of silver, and for all manner of work to be made by the hands of artificers. And who then is willing to consecrate his service this day unto the LORD?*
>
> (1 Chronicles 29:5)

Service is definitely one aspect of consecration. Basically, it should be worship "who is willing." God presents an opportunity to us to offer ourselves to Him. God will never cross the threshold of human responsibility.

"Willing to consecrate" consecration is an act of the will. I must make a decision. Consecration is abdicating the rulership of our lives in favor of King Jesus.

The "I" yields to the authority of Christ as Master. Who is boss in your life?

A personal example of consecration may be seen in Abraham's life.

To leave a country and kindred.

Now the Lord had said unto Abram, Get thee out of thy country, and from thy kindred, and from they father's house, unto a land that I will shew thee.

(Genesis 12:1)

Separation from Lot.

Is not the whole land before thee? separate thyself, I pray thee, from me: if thou wilt take the left hand, then I will go to the right; or if thou depart to the right hand, then I will go to the left.

(Genesis 13:9)

Cast out Hagar and Ishmael.

Wherefore she said unto Abraham, Cast out this bondwoman and her sons: for the son of this bondwoman shall not be heir with my son, even with Isaac.

(Genesis 21:10)

Offering of Isaac.

And he said, Take now thy son, thine only son Isaac, whom thou lovest, and get thee into the land of Moriah; and offer him there for a burnt offering upon one of the mountains which I will tell thee of.

(Genesis 22:2)

I. What is consecration?

Consecration involves two acts.

Yielding my will to God, the presentation of myself to Christ for His glory.

Consecration is the act of God when He accepts the sacrifice that I make.

The priests did not consecrate themselves. Aaron and his sons merely yielded.

Consecration involves devoting oneself to God.

Arise and thresh, O daughter of Zion: for I will make thine horn iron, and I will make thy hoofs brass: and thou shalt beat in pieces many people: and I will consecrate their gain unto the Lord, and their substance unto the Lord of the whole earth.

(Micah 4:13)

It involves separation unto God.

And he shall consecrate unto the LORD the days of his separation, and shall bring a lamb of the first year for a trespass offering: but the days that were before shall be lost, because his separation was defiled.

(Numbers 6:12)

II. Who can be consecrated?

Those that are cleansed by the blood of Christ may be eligible for consecration. Those who are members of God's family are invited to consecrate themselves.

Consecration is not exclusive to the great, mighty or talented, but is open to every believer.

I beseech you therefore, brethren, by the mercies of God, that ye present your bodies a living sacri-

*fice, holy, acceptable unto God, which is your rea-
sonable service.*

(Romans 12:1)

III. The appeal to consecration:

"...by the mercies of God..." **(Romans 12:1).**

We are not commanded to come by force or authority
but by His mercies. Our consecration is not prompted by
fear, but by love and mercy.

Some of God's mercies: justification, identification, sanctification, indwelling of the Holy Spirit, no condemnation,
daily help, heaven after death, health, friends, church.

IV. The act of consecration:

"...present your bodies..." **(Romans 12:1).**

1. It is voluntary. Paul makes a beseeching, pleading
call or invitation. It is like giving a present. We are not
forced to do it.

2. It is personal. *"Your* bodies." This means our lives,
everything that we have.

3. It is sacrificial, a living sacrifice. It is putting our
lives on the altar, as Abraham presented Isaac.

This reasonable presentation of ourselves to God surely
delights the heart of our Father. The earthly father is hurt
if the child reluctantly draws back from him. The child
accepts the father's protection, food and clothes, but the
father also desires the child's intimate fellowship.

I believe this act is a supreme act of worship.

And Abraham said unto his young men, Abide ye here with the ass; and I and the lad will go yonder and worship, and come again to you.
(Genesis 22:5)

V. The argument for consecration:

"...reasonable service" (Romans 12:1).

If we have been truly redeemed, then it is only reasonable that we give Him our puny service.

Intelligent Christianity lends itself to service gladly and unreservedly. God's service is not unreasonable. It is the only sensible thing to do.

If we consider it for a moment there can be no other conclusion. Maybe we say that it is too hard. It was hard for the Father to part with the Son. It was hard for Abraham to offer Isaac. The life of Joseph was hard.

It was hard to leave the comforts of Pharaoh's palace. It was hard for Job to lose all. It was hard for Paul to witness at Rome and Ephesus, but it was the will of God, and they accepted it.

VI. What am I to consecrate?

"Your bodies."

1. My body must be given to Him to use as He desires, whereby He may get more glory. Our bodies are not our own. They have been redeemed by Christ with His blood. Give Him your physical strength. Praise God for health and use it for Him.

77

2. Give Him your feet to run errands of mercy to take the Gospel to someone. Give Him your hands to do works of benevolence and lift the fallen.

Give Him your eyes to seek out the needy and perishing. Give Him your ears to hear the cry of the distressed and seek then for Him. Give Him your time. He must govern the use of your time. Let Him arrange the program.

Interruptions then will come from Him. My study time, my work time, my play time must be counted as sacred. Let Him guide you moment by moment in this matter.

"Redeeming the time, because the days are evil" (Ephesians 5:16).

"Walk in wisdom toward them that are without, redeeming the time" (Colossians 4:5).

3. Give Him your talents. Whether you have one or two or five or ten talents, let them all be for Him.

Ability to speak, to preach, to teach, to minister the Word of God. Ability to sing, play an instrument, lead a choir or an orchestra for His glory. Ability to write books, poems, articles, Christian stories. Write for Him.

Ability to pray, to be an intercessor, a prayer warrior. One of the greatest talents. Ability of leadership and organization. This is much needed in the Church today. Ability to be a good follower, to assist others, to carry out programs.

Ability to be manifested in your vocation: nurse, teacher, electrician, shopkeeper.

4. Give Him your possessions. We gladly present to Him our gold, silver, all that we possess. Not only give Him the tithe but give Him everything.

5. Give Him your heart. This is what He wants more than anything else. The heart is symbolic of the inner man, the real self. *"...But first gave their own selves to the Lord..."* (2 Corinthians 8:5). Consecration means giving everything that I have to the Lord, but giving myself first.

VII. The results of consecration:

1. Is a life that is not conformed to this world. It is a not a worldly, selfish life.

2. A life that is transformed by the renewed mind. The renewed man thinks as God thinks, with eternal values in view.

3. A life lived harmoniously in the will of God happily following His plan.

4. A life that is acceptable. God's will is never obnoxious. This life will surely be acceptable both by God and by man.

5. A life that is good. It will be beneficial. Never fear the consequences of consecration. Men and women will rise up and call you blessed because you obeyed God.

6. A life that is happy, joyous, victorious, because it was lived in the perfect will of God, the One who created you and redeemed you with His precious blood.

Conclusion:

Consecration is a process. It is daily, and moment by moment yielding in the daily crisis. The daily renewal of our consecration is not by the flesh but by the indwelling Spirit. Never take it back. A gift is given to be reclaimed no more.

Review Questions:

1. What do we learn about consecration from *"The gold for things of gold, and the silver for things of silver, and for all manner of work to be made by the hands of artificers. And who then is willing to consecrate his service this day unto the LORD"* (1 Chronicles 29:5)?

2. What is the basic purpose of consecration?

3. Name the two acts involved in consecration.

4. Who is eligible to make an acceptable consecration?

5. What is the New Testament appeal to consecration based on?

6. What three things do we learn about consecration from *"I beseech you therefore, brethren, by the mercies of God, that ye present your bodies a living sacrifice, holy, acceptable unto God, which is your reasonable service"* (Romans 12:1)?

7. If consecration is difficult, does that mean that it is unreasonable? Why?

CHILDREN OF ADOPTION

Introduction:

Regeneration begins a new life in the soul when it is born again by the Spirit. Justification deals with the new attitude of God towards that soul. Adoption admits man into the family of God with filial joy to our Father God.

Regeneration is a changed nature; justification is a changed standing; sanctification is a changed character; while adoption is a changed position.

In regeneration the believer becomes a child of God; in adoption the child receives the position of an adult son; the baby or minor becomes an adult.

> *To redeem them that were under the law, that we might receive the adoption of sons.*
> (Galatians 4:5)

> *Wherefore thou art no more a servant, but a son; and if a son, then an heir of God through Christ.*
> (Galatians 4:7)

Adoption is our growing up in Christ and occupying our new position. Here are two questions for each of us to ponder.

1. Is this standing instantaneous with conversion?

2. Can the adopted son be disinherited and cast away for being a prodigal?

I. The meaning of adoption

"Adoption" is a Greek word which means, "The placing of a son."

For ye have not received the spirit of bondage again to fear; but ye have received the Spirit of adoption, whereby we cry, Abba, Father.
(Romans 8:15)

Having predestinated us unto the adoption of children by Jesus Christ to Himself, according to the good pleasure of His will.
(Ephesians 1:5)

In Bible times the word had a twofold meaning:

1. The private act of receiving a stranger into the family as a son.

2. The public, legal, ceremonial act of recognizing the son as the heir; something like a coming out or coming of age party.

Until this ceremony was performed the child actually differed little from servants in the home. The Word deals not with our relationship with God but our position before Him.

Adoption is the act of God whereby He places the justified believer as an adult son to enjoy the privileges and responsibilities of the position.

In Exodus 2 Moses became the adopted son of Pharaoh's daughter with all the rights and privileges of that position when he came of age.

By faith Moses, when he was come to years, refused to be called the son of Pharaoh's daughter.

(Hebrews 11:24)

Moses rejected his Egyptian position for something better.

II. The condition of adoption:

Adoption has only one condition and that is to abide in Christ, in union with Him.

For ye are all the children of God by faith in Christ Jesus.

(Galatians 3:26)

We do not have to wait until we have been a saint for one year or ten years, but immediately we enter into all the blessings of a fully recognized heir of God.

III. The time of adoption:

1. It occurred before the foundation of the world.

For the children being not yet born, neither having done any good or evil, that the purpose of God according to election might stand, not of works, but of him that calleth.

(Romans 9:11)

Adoption is a gracious act on the part of God entirely out of mercy; we do not deserve nor merit this loving favor from a holy God.

2. It actually occurs the moment that one believes in Jesus Christ.

Beloved, now are we the sons of God, and it doth not yet appear what we shall be: but we know that, when He shall appear, we shall be like Him; for we shall see Him as He is.

(1 John 3:2)

Sonship is a present possession.

We can truthfully say, "I'm a child of the King, not His slave, but His son and heir." We are not mere children under maids and tutors, but adult members of the family.

3. Adoption will be completed at the resurrection when we enter His presence.

And not only they, but ourselves also, which have the firstfruits of the Spirit, even we ourselves groan within ourselves, waiting for the adoption, to wit, the redemption of our body.

(Romans 8:23)

Guidance by the Holy Spirit is the path to sonship and the proof of sonship. The Holy Spirit guides the believer into the truth of God.

Howbeit when He, the Spirit of truth, is come, He will guide you into all truth: for He shall not speak of Himself; but whatsoever He shall hear, that shall He speak: and He will shew you things to come.

(John 16:13)

But if ye be led of the Spirit, ye are not under the law.

(Galatians 5:18)

V. The cry of adoption:

*For ye have not received the spirit of bondage
again to fear; but ye have received the Spirit of
adoption, whereby we cry, Abba, Father.*
(Romans 8:15)

*And because ye are sons, God hath sent forth the
Spirit of His Son into your hearts, crying, Abba,
Father.*
(Galatians 4:6)

*And he said, Abba, Father, all things are possible
unto thee; take away this cup from me: nevertheless not what I will, but what thou wilt.*
(Mark 14:36)

This is a special word of endearment of close relationship. "ABBA" is Aramaic, the language of Christ's childhood. "Father" is a Greek word, the language of the educated and learned of His day. A slave was never allowed to
address him as "Abba."

VI. The blessings of adoption:

1. They become objects of God's peculiar love.

*I in them, and Thou in me, that they may be
made perfect in one; and that the world may
know that Thou hast sent me, and hast loved
them, as Thou hast loved me.*
(John 17:23)

2. They become objects of the Father's fatherly care.
The Father God looks after their livelihood as to what
they will and wear; their occupation and health.

3. They have the family name.

Behold, what manner of love the Father hath bestowed upon us, that we should be called the sons of God: therefore the world knoweth us not, because it knew Him not.

(1 John 3:1)

4. They have the family likeness.

For whom He did foreknow, He also did predestinate to be conformed to the image of His Son, that He might be the firstborn among many brethren.

(Romans 8:29)

They have the family love.

We know that we have passed from death unto life, because we love the brethren. He that loveth not his brother abideth in death.

(1 John 3:14)

They have the filial spirit.

For ye have not received the spirit of bondage again to fear; but ye have received the Spirit of adoption, whereby we cry, Abba, Father.

(Romans 8:15)

The parent-child relationship.

They have the family gathering.

Jesus answered and said unto him, If a man love Me, he will keep My words: and My Father will love him, and We will come unto him, and make Our abode with him.

(John 14:23)

86

They receive fatherly chastisement.

And ye have forgotten the exhortation which speaketh unto you as unto children, My son, despise not thou the chastening of the Lord, nor faint when thou art rebuked of Him: For whom the Lord loveth He chasteneth, and scourgeth every son whom He receiveth. If ye endure chastening, God dealeth with you as with sons; for what son is he whom the father chasteneth not? But if ye be without chastisement, whereof all are partakers, then are ye bastards, and not sons. Furthermore we have had fathers of our flesh which corrected us, and we gave them reverence: shall we not much rather be in subjection unto the Father of spirits, and live? For they verily for a few days chastened us after their own pleasure; but He for our profit, that we might be partakers of His holiness. Now no chastening for the present seemeth to be joyous, but grievous: nevertheless afterward it yieldeth the peaceable fruit of righteousness unto them which are exercised thereby.

(Hebrews 12:5-11)

They receive fatherly comfort.

Who comforteth us in all our tribulation, that we may be able to comfort them which are in any trouble, by the comfort wherewith we ourselves are comforted of God.

(2 Corinthians 1:4)

They receive the Father's inheritance.

To an inheritance incorruptible, and undefiled,

and that fadeth not away, reserved in heaven for you.

(1 Peter 1:4)

VII. The responsibility of adoption:

Members of the royal family of heaven must behave with becoming dignity. We are to walk worthy of this high honor in keeping with our position. We must love and serve one another as brothers and sisters in the same family.

If I then, your Lord and Master, have washed your feet; ye also ought to wash one another's feet.

(John 13:14)

These things I command you, that ye love one another.

(John 15:17)

Conclusion:

As a child enjoys the free run of the house and the privileges of running into the Father's presence at any time, so does the believer approach God's presence.

Those who are adopted into the family of God are led by the Spirit of God.

Am I led by the Holy Spirit? Do I have the childlike confidence in my Father? Do I avail myself of this liberty of access into His very own presence? Do I love the brethren, the family of God, as I ought to? Am I a filial son? Am I obedient to the commands that He has given me?

Let us leave our spiritual babyhood and assume our position of manhood in Christ. We ought to possess our possessions and lives as son of God; heirs of God.

Sometimes when parents adopt a child they try to keep that fact a secret from their children lest they will feel less than a full son or daughter.

The story is told of one child, who knew that he was adopted, being teased by another child: "You are just an adopted child," with the inference that he was probably illegitimate or something.

However, the boy was proud of being adopted and replied, "Yes, I'm adopted. My parents chose me, picked me out of many babies. Your parents had to take what they got." It is true that we are adopted into God's family; He chose us, praise His name.

Review Questions:

1. Distinguish between regeneration, justification, and adoption.

2. Give the two Palestinian meanings of adoption and its present Scriptural meaning.

3. What is the condition of adoption?

4. Give the three tenses of adoption with one Scripture for each.

5. What is the sign that an individual is adopted into the family of God?

6. Explain, "Abba, Father."

7. List seven blessings of adoption.

8. What is the relationship between Hebrews 12:5-11 and adoption?

9. What is the responsibility of an adopted son (or daughter) to God?

10. What is the blessed privilege of an adopted son?

About the Author

Irose Fernella Thompson was born in Antique West Indies to George Adams, deceased, and Mary Adams-Davis. She is the oldest of ten children. She is a born-again Christian who enjoys doing the service of the King. She has one son, and his family who reside in Maplewood, New Jersey. In December of 1999, she married the late Bishop Thompson and has extended her family with the addition of four step-children and grandchildren. She is a retired nurse from the Veterans Medical Center, East Orange, NJ. She earned a Bachelor of Theology from United Bible College in Orlando, Florida, a Master of Theology from Jamison Bible College in Puerto Rico, and is the recipient of an honorary Doctorate degree from Gracehill Tabernacle College in Newark, New Jersey.

In 1984, she published her first book, *Faith Hope and Love* with Vantage Press in New York. She enjoys writing poetry and has publications in various anthologies. She is also published in *Marqui's Who's Who in America*. Above all, she cherishes the gift of the Holy Ghost that enables her to accomplish her God-given assignments.

BIBLIOGRAPHY

Coon, Dennis: *Introduction To Psychology*, West Publishing Company, St. Paul, MN, Copyright 1986.

[1] Coon, Dennis, *Introduction to Psychology*, pg. 459